The Therapeutic Techniques

A step by step guide on

How to recover, overcome and break free from PTSD

Aldous Ashia Adjei

Table of Content

Chapter 1: Understanding Complex PTSD

In the faintly lit hallways of our minds, shadows cast by past injuries frequently wait concealed, forming our display encounters in significant but regularly unnoticed ways. Understanding Complex PTSD (Post-Traumatic Stress Disorder) is associated with setting out on an endeavour into these covered up breaks, where the echoes of past torment resound and interlace with our day by day lives.

Unlike the more commonplace PTSD, which regularly emerges from single, traumatic occasions, Complex PTSD emerges from drawn out introduction to injury, regularly starting in childhood or proceeding over extended periods in adulthood. This shape of PTSD doesn't fairly affect how people respond to particular triggers but penetrates their whole worldview, self-image, and relationships.

Imagine an embroidered artwork woven with strings of fear, disgrace, and detachment, each strand a memory or involvement that has formed the person's mental scene. Complex PTSD weaves these strings firmly, making a complex design of passionate triggers, shirking behaviours, and strongly enthusiastic reactions that can perplex both the sufferer and those around them.

Central to understanding Complex PTSD is recognizing its multifaceted indications. People may battle with passionate dysregulation, finding themselves swaying between overpowering sentiments of fear, outrage, or deadness. They might fight with determined sentiments of disgrace and uselessness, established in encounters of disregard, manhandle, or disloyalty. Connections, as well, ended up battlegrounds where designs of evasion, doubt, or codependency play out, reflecting the social wounds of their past.

Yet, inside the shadows, there is moreover resilience—a calm quality that perseveres in spite of misfortune. Survivors of Complex PTSD frequently show surprising boldness in going up against their injury, looking for understanding, and producing ways towards mending. They explore the overly complex passages of their minds with specialists, revealing buried recollections and reframing their stories from ones of victimhood to stories of survival and resilience.

In this chapter, we start our travel by shedding light on the nature of Complex PTSD—its roots, signs, and significant impacts on individuals' lives. We dive into the science behind injury, investigating how delayed push modifies brain work, sustaining cycles of trouble and evasion. Through compelling stories and master bits of knowledge, we welcome perusers to peer into the shadows and go up against the complexities of this often-misunderstood condition.

Ultimately, this chapter sets the arrange for the transformative travel ahead. It challenges us to see past surface indications and stand up to the more profound wounds that shape our lives. By understanding Complex PTSD, we not as it were to light up the way to recuperation but to honour the versatility and mettle of those who walk it.

Chapter 2: How Trauma Shapes Our Lives

Imagine dropping a stone into a quiet pond not a raging sea—the beginning sprinkle is fair the starting. Swells cascade outward, touching everything in their way, changing the surface of the water. Essentially, injury, especially in its complex frame, acts as that stone, sending out waves that resound through each perspective of our lives.

At its centre, injury disturbs our sense of security and security, taking off permanent marks on our mind. For those hooked with Complex PTSD, these impacts amplify distant past the introductory traumatic occasions, impacting considerations, feelings, behaviours, and connections in significant ways.

The swell impact of injury starts inside, reshaping the exceptional scene of our minds. Survivors frequently discover themselves caught in cycles of hyperarousal or separation, where increased watchfulness and flashbacks obscure the boundaries between past and display. Uneasiness and discouragement may become consistent companions, their beginnings established in encounters of weakness or betrayal.

Externally, injury changes how we explore the world and relate to others. It can dissolve belief, making closeness feel perilous and defenselessness agonising. Designs of shirking or self-sabotage may rise as adapting instruments, securing against seen dangers but moreover separating us from potential sources of bolster and connection.

Moreover, the swell impact amplifies past person encounters to shape broader social flow. Families, communities, and social orders bear witness to the consequence of injury, hooked with its effect on connections, social standards, and social stories. In understanding how injury shapes our lives, we stand up not as it were individually enduring but to the collective challenge of cultivating strength and recuperating inside our communities.

Yet, in the midst of the turbulence of trauma's swell impact, there exists strength and trust. Survivors illustrate uncommon quality in exploring these turbulent waters, looking for understanding, and recovering office over their lives. Helpful intercessions, from cognitive-behavioural procedures to physical encounter, offer pathways to recuperating by tending to the complex transaction of contemplations, feelings, and real sensations.

In this chapter, we investigate the far-reaching results of injury, lighting up how its swell impact saturates each feature of our presence. Through compelling stories and master experiences, we dive into the neuroscience of injury, revealing how stretch changes brain work and propagates cycles of trouble. We moreover celebrate the strength of survivors, highlighting their ventures towards recovering independence and manufacturing important connections.

PTSD

The chapter welcomes perusers to mull over the interconnecting of injury and strength, challenging us to recognize the transformative control of mending. By understanding how injury shapes our lives, we honour the boldness of survivors and develop sympathy inside ourselves and our communities.

Chapter 3: Knowing The Triggers of PTSD

Imagine standing at the edge of an endless, dim abyss—an pit that speaks to the profundities of enthusiastic triggers implanted inside the mind of somebody with Complex PTSD. Each trigger is like a gravitational drive, pulling us into the profundities of fear, disgrace, or lost hope, where past wounds throb with difficult resonance.

Emotional triggers are not simple recollections; they are entries through which the past penetrates the display, mutilating discernments and forces passionate reactions. For people with Complex PTSD, apparently harmless sights, sounds, or circumstances can inspire visceral responses, unleashing downpours of feeling that oppose level headed explanation.

Navigating these enthusiastic voids requires boldness and understanding. It requests an eagerness to go up against the shadows of injury, to disentangle the tangled strings of past encounters that proceed to apply their hold on the display. Treatment gets to be a voyage of discovery—a travel into the heart of haziness where mending starts with understanding.

Therapeutic modalities such as EMDR (Eye Development Desensitization and Reprocessing) or argumentative behaviour treatment offer devices for exploring these passionate profundities. They give systems for handling injury, developing enthusiastic direction, and cultivating flexibility in the confrontation of triggers that once appeared insurmountable.

Yet, the journey into the chasm is not single. It is guided by compassionate specialists, strong partners, and individual travellers who bear witness to our battles and celebrate our triumphs. Together, we make secure harbours where powerlessness is met with compassion, and recuperating gets to be a shared endeavour.

In this chapter, we dive into the pit of passionate triggers, investigating their roots, appearances, and transformative potential. Through strong stories and master points of view, we light up the perplexing web of triggers that trap survivors of Complex PTSD, advertising bits of knowledge into how treatment and self-awareness can lead to freedom from their grip.

This challenges us to stand up to our most profound wounds with strength and sympathy. By exploring the enthusiastic triggers that characterise our ventures, we recover organisation over our feelings and fashion pathways to mending. This chapter welcomes perusers to grasp powerlessness as a catalyst for change, recognizing that inside the profundities of injury lies the guarantee of versatility and reestablishment.

Chapter 4: Rediscovering Yourself In the midst of Trauma

Imagine a mosaic smashed by a sudden impact—the pieces scattered, each part carrying a sea of the entire. For survivors of Complex PTSD, injury breaks the sense of self, clearing out behind a smashed personality formed by difficulty and survival.

At the heart of recuperation lies the travel to recovering identity—a handle both overwhelming and freeing. It starts with standing up to the divided self, piecing together the shards of identity and memory that injury has scattered. Each part tells a story—a story of flexibility, adjustment, and survival in the confrontation of overpowering adversity.

PTSD

Trauma mutilates self-perception, regularly clearing out people with Complex PTSD feeling detached from their genuine selves. They may battle with significant sentiments of vacancy or an unavoidable sense of being on a very basic level imperfect. Character gets to be a battleground where clashing viewpoints of the self—survivor and casualty, quality and vulnerability—clash and intertwine.

Therapeutic investigation gets to be a journey for coherence—a travel to coordinate these divided perspectives into a cohesive sense of self. Procedures such as story treatment or mindfulness-based homes offer pathways to self-discovery, permitting people to modify their accounts from ones of victimhood to stories of strengthening and resilience.

Moreover, recovering personality includes grasping the complexity of lived encounters. It requires recognizing the scars of injury whereas celebrating the qualities fashioned in its pot. Through self-compassion and acknowledgment, survivors develop a more profound understanding of who they are past their traumatic histories.

In this chapter, we dive into the significant travel of recovering character in the midst of injury. Through reminiscent stories and restorative bits of knowledge, we investigate the transformative control of self-discovery and self-acceptance. We enlighten the challenges of exploring personality in the repercussions of injury and celebrate the strength of those who set out on this bold path.

This chapter welcomes perusers to reflect on their claim ventures of self-discovery, recognizing that mending from Complex PTSD includes more than indication management—it requires recovering organisation over one's story and grasping the multifaceted layers of personality formed by strength and development.

Chapter 5: Mending from Disloyalty and Abandonment

Imagine a sensitive embroidered artwork woven from strings of believe and association, each strand defenceless to the scarcest shred. For people with Complex PTSD, encounters of disloyalty and deserting regularly smash these bonds, taking off behind rugged edges of torment and doubt that reverberate through connections and self-perception.

Betrayal cuts deep—it undermines our sense of security and breaks our capacity to believe others. Whether it stems from manhandle, disregard, or broken guarantees, selling out takes off enthusiastic wounds that can putrefy for a long time, forming how we see ourselves and associated with the world.

Similarly, deserting echoes through the passages of our mind, taking off behind a frequenting sense of unworthiness or fear of dismissal. Whether through physical nonattendance or enthusiastic inaccessibility, surrender disturbs connection bonds, clearing out people with Complex PTSD exploring a scene scarred by misfortune and longing.

Healing from disloyalty and deserting is a multifaceted journey—one that starts with recognizing the profundity of passionate torment and the ways it has moulded our social designs. Helpful intercessions, such as attachment-focused treatment or interpersonal psychotherapy, offer systems for investigating these wounds, cultivating recuperating through compassionate investigation and reconnection.

Moreover, recuperating requires developing self-compassion and forgiveness—both towards others and ourselves. It includes recognizing that the scars of selling out and deserting do not characterise us but serve as confirmations to our versatility and capacity for growth.

In this chapter, we dive into the complex flow of recuperating from selling out and surrender. Through piercing stories and helpful experiences, we investigate the significant effect of these encounters on individuals' lives and connections. We celebrate the strength of survivors who stand up to these wounds with helplessness and kindness, fashioning pathways to recover belief, and modify important connections.

This chapter welcomes perusers to reflect on their possess encounters of disloyalty and deserting, recognizing the transformative control of recuperating and absolution. By exploring these enthusiastic scenes, we honour the flexibility of the human soul and develop compassion towards ourselves and others on the journey towards recuperating.

Chapter 6: Rebuilding Connections After Trauma

Imagine embarking on a journey through a dense forest, where every step requires courage and resilience. This journey symbolises the road to trust for individuals grappling with Complex PTSD—a path fraught with obstacles yet illuminated by the possibility of healing and connection.

Trust, once shattered by trauma, becomes a precious commodity—a fragile thread that binds individuals to others and to themselves. Whether betrayed by caregivers, peers, or intimate partners, survivors often confront a daunting landscape of fear, suspicion, and vulnerability in their relationships.

Rebuilding trust begins with understanding the origins of relational wounds. Therapy becomes a sanctuary—a safe space where survivors can explore the impact of past betrayals and abandonment on their ability to trust. Through compassionate guidance and therapeutic interventions like schema therapy or relational psychotherapy, individuals learn to distinguish between past threats and present realities, reclaiming agency over their relational narratives.

Yet, the road to trust is not linear. It requires navigating internal landscapes marked by ambivalence, fear, and longing for connection. Survivors may grapple with oscillating between closeness and withdrawal, testing the waters of vulnerability while guarding against potential harm.

Moreover, rebuilding trust involves cultivating self-trust—a process of honouring one's intuition, needs, and boundaries with compassion and authenticity. It requires acknowledging the resilience forged through adversity and embracing the inherent worthiness of seeking connection and support.

In this chapter, we explore the transformative journey of rebuilding trust after trauma. Through evocative narratives and therapeutic insights, we illuminate the complexities of trust dynamics in relationships affected by Complex PTSD. We celebrate the resilience of survivors who embark on this courageous path, honouring their capacity for growth and healing.

We invites readers to reflect on their own journeys of trust and connection, recognizing that healing from trauma involves more than rebuilding broken bonds—it requires reclaiming agency over one's relational landscape and embracing the transformative power of vulnerability and authenticity.

Chapter 7: Embracing Healing Through Acceptance

Imagine standing on the edge of a precipice, overlooking a vast expanse of uncertainty. This image encapsulates the essence of courageous vulnerability—the willingness to confront our deepest wounds with openness and compassion, even when the path ahead seems daunting and uncertain.

For individuals with Complex PTSD, healing often begins with embracing courageous vulnerability—a paradoxical journey that demands both strength and surrender. It involves confronting the rawness of emotional pain, acknowledging the scars left by trauma, and allowing ourselves to be seen and supported in our struggles.

Courageous vulnerability requires dismantling the armor we've erected to protect ourselves from further harm. It challenges the belief that vulnerability equates to weakness, inviting us instead to recognize it as a profound act of courage—a testament to our resilience and capacity for growth.

Therapy becomes a crucible for courageous vulnerability—a safe space where survivors can explore their innermost fears and insecurities with compassionate guidance. Therapeutic modalities such as mindfulness-based practices, somatic experiencing, or expressive arts therapy offer tools for cultivating self-awareness and fostering acceptance of our vulnerabilities.

Moreover, embracing courageous vulnerability involves extending compassion towards ourselves. It requires reframing self-judgement and perfectionism as barriers to healing, recognizing that true growth emerges from a place of self-acceptance and self-compassion.

In this chapter, we delve into the transformative power of courageous vulnerability in the journey towards healing from Complex PTSD. Through evocative narratives and therapeutic insights, we explore the nuances of embracing vulnerability as a catalyst for personal growth and connection. We celebrate the courage of survivors who navigate the depths of their emotional landscapes with openness and authenticity, forging pathways to profound healing and self-discovery.

We invites readers to reflect on their own relationships with vulnerability and self-acceptance, recognizing that healing from trauma involves embracing all facets of our humanity with courage and compassion. By honouring the transformative power of vulnerability, we honour the resilience and strength inherent within each of us on the journey towards wholeness.

Chapter 8: From Survival to Thriving: Cultivating Adaptability and Growth

Imagine a seedling arising from rich soil, reaching towards the sun with unvarying determination. This image embodies the substance of adaptability — a dynamic process of adoption and growth in response to adversity. For individualities with Complex PTSD, cultivating adaptability isn't just about surviving trauma but thriving in its fate.

Adaptability is the capacity to bounce back from lapses, to navigate challenges with inflexibility and strength. It emerges from a complex interplay of particular strengths, external supports, and adaptive managing strategies that enable individualities to repel and indeed transcend the impact of trauma.

At its core, cultivating adaptability involves reclaiming agency over one's narrative. It requires reframing guests of adversity as openings for growth and literacy, rather than invincible obstacles. remedial interventions similar as adaptability- concentrated remedy or trauma-informed care offer fabrics for fostering adaptability by empowering individualities to harness their ingrained strengths and coffers.

Also, adaptability thrives within probative connections and communities. Connection becomes a lifeline — a source of confirmation, stimulant, and collective understanding that sustains individualities through their mending trip. Peer support groups, community networks, and remedial alliances give spaces where survivors can partake their stories, find solidarity, and cultivate adaptability together.

In this chapter, we explore the transformative trip from survival to thriving amidst Complex PTSD. Through compelling narratives and expert perceptivity, we illuminate the dynamics of adaptability — its origins, instantiations, and pathways to civilization. We celebrate the adaptability of survivors who navigate the complications of trauma with courage and determination, recognizing their capacity for growth, mending, and commission.

" From Survival to Thriving" invites compendiums to reflect on their own peregrinations of adaptability and growth, feting that mending from trauma involves further than prostrating adversity — it involves embracing adaptability as a guiding force towards reclaiming agency, chancing purpose, and fostering meaningful connections. By recognizing the transformative power of adaptability, we recognize the insuperable spirit within each of us on the path towards thriving.

Chapter 9: Changing Torment into Empathy

Imagine a tender rain shower feeding dried soil, bringing life to torpid seeds and cultivating development. This picture epitomises the transformative control of compassion—a significant constraint that recuperates not as it were ourselves but moreover those around us. For people with Complex PTSD, developing sympathy is an imperative pathway towards recuperating and connection.

Compassion starts with recognizing the profundity of our possessiveness, enduring with benevolence and understanding. It includes grasping the injured parts of ourselves with delicacy, or maybe than judgement or self-blame. Through treatment and mindfulness homes, people learn to develop self-compassion—a home that cultivates strength and advances enthusiastic healing.

Moreover, kindness amplifies past the self—it includes bearing witness to the enduring of others with sympathy and nearness. Survivors of Complex PTSD frequently have an increased affectability to the torment of others, stemming from their claim encounters of injury and misfortune. This empathic attunement gets to be a catalyst for building important associations and cultivating mending inside relationships.

In restorative settings, compassion-focused treatments and mindfulness-based intercessions offer apparatuses for developing compassion and cultivating recuperating through interpersonal association. Homes such as loving-kindness contemplation or account treatment empower people to investigate their social elements with sympathy and interest, changing torment into pathways for development and understanding.

In this chapter, we dive into the significant control of sympathy in the setting of Complex PTSD. Through reminiscent stories and restorative bits of knowledge, we investigate how developing self-compassion and sympathy can clear the way towards mending and flexibility. We celebrate the strength of survivors who saddle the transformative potential of kindness, both for themselves and others, cultivating association and advancing recuperating inside their communities.

This chapter welcomes perusers to reflect on their claim connections with self-compassion and compassion, recognizing that recuperating from injury includes grasping sympathy as a foundation of versatility and association. By honouring the transformative control of sympathy, we honour the capacity for recuperating and development inalienable inside each of us on the journey towards wholeness.

Chapter 10: Lighting the Way Tools and Strategies for Long- Term Recovery

Imagine standing at a crossroads, girdled by multiple paths leading towards mending and growth. This image encapsulates the substance of Chapter 10 — a guidebook filled with practical tools, strategies, and perceptivity designed to illuminate the trip of long- term recovery from Complex PTSD.

Recovery isn't a destination but an ongoing process — a trip of tone- discovery, mending, and metamorphosis. It requires a multifaceted approach that addresses the complex interplay of cerebral, emotional, and relational factors impacted by trauma.

Central to long- term recovery is the integration of remedial modalities that empower individualities to recapture control over their lives. Cognitive- behavioural ways help challenge distorted study patterns and actions embedded in trauma, fostering adaptability and promoting adaptive managing strategies.

Likewise, physical passing and awareness- grounded practices offer pathways to reconnecting mind and body, cultivating mindfulness of physiological responses to stress and trauma. These practices grease mending by promoting tone- regulation and reducing the impact of traumatic recollections on diurnal functioning.

In addition to individual remedy, support networks play a pivotal part in sustaining long- term recovery. Peer support groups, community coffers, and online forums give spaces for confirmation, participating guests , and collective support. These networks offer solidarity and stimulants, reminding individuals that they aren't alone on their trip towards mending.

Also, self-care becomes a foundation of long- term recovery — a practice that encompasses nurturing physical health, prioritising rest and relaxation, and engaging in conditioning that brings joy and fulfilment. By prioritising self-care, individualities replenish their reserves of adaptability and cultivate a sense of commission in their recovery trip.

In this chapter, we explore a comprehensive toolkit of tools and strategies for long- term recovery from Complex PTSD. Through practical advice, particular stories, and expert guidance, we empower compendiums to navigate the complications of trauma with adaptability and determination. We celebrate the transformative power of recovery, recognizing the courage and perseverance of individualities who embark on this trip towards mending and wholeness.

"Lighting the Way" invites compendiums to reflect on their own recovery processes, feeling that mending from trauma involves embracing a holistic approach that integrates remedial interventions, support networks, and tone- care practices. By illuminating the path towards long- term recovery, we empower individuals to reclaim their lives, foster meaningful connections, and cultivate adaptability in the face of adversity.

Conclusion

All in all, the outing of understanding and recuperating from Complex PTSD is a significant investigation of unbending nature, repairing, and change. All through this book, we have scooped into the mind boggling elements of injury's effect on independences' lives, associations, and feelings of self. We have enlightened the way towards retouching with sympathy, compassion, and viable instruments intended to engage and direct.

Every part has offered perceptivity into the confusions of injury — from the first unearthing of murk to exploring close to home triggers, recovering personality, and remaking trust. We have investigated the extraordinary force of manful weakness, the inflexibility that rises up out of misfortune, and the retouching possibility of empathy — both for us and others.

Likewise, we have outfitted collections with an extensive tool compartment for long haul recuperation, stressing the meaning of incorporating healing modalities, developing encouraging groups of people, and focusing on self-care. By embracing these systems, distinctions can recover organisation over their stories, encourage significant associations, and develop unbending nature despite difficulty.

Eventually, this book is a respect to the mental fortitude and unbending nature of overcomers of Intricate PTSD. It praises their campaigns towards repairing and development, commending their ability to rise above torment and recover their lives. By slipping light on the groundbreaking force of figuring out, empathy, and self-discovery, we desire to motivate and enable collections in their own ways towards repairing and completeness.

May this journey of investigation and commission act as a signal of convenience and direction for every one of those exploring the confusions of injury. As we keep on learning, developing, and supporting each other, may we encourage networks of sympathy, inflexibility, and patching that insist the fundamental strength and quality inside each exist.